support.

In love and light

Janice ♡

Make Me a Channel of *your Words*

Past, Future, **NOW**

Channelled through JANICE THOMSON

BALBOA.PRESS

A DIVISION OF HAY HOUSE

Balboa Press books may be ordered through booksellers or by contacting:

Balboa Press
A Division of Hay House
1663 Liberty Drive
Bloomington, IN 47403
www.balboapress.co.uk
UK TFN: 0800 0148647 (Toll Free inside the UK)
UK Local: (02) 0369 56325 (+44 20 3695 6325 from outside the UK)

Because of the dynamic nature of the Internet, any web addresses or links contained in this book may have changed since publication and may no longer be valid. The views expressed in this work are solely those of the author and do not necessarily reflect the views of the publisher, and the publisher hereby disclaims any responsibility for them.

The author of this book does not dispense medical advice or prescribe the use of any technique as a form of treatment for physical, emotional, or medical problems without the advice of a physician, either directly or indirectly. The intent of the author is only to offer information of a general nature to help you in your quest for emotional and spiritual well-being. In the event you use any of the information in this book for yourself, which is your constitutional right, the author and the publisher assume no responsibility for your actions.

Any people depicted in stock imagery provided by Getty Images are models, and such images are being used for illustrative purposes only. Certain stock imagery © Getty Images.

Print information available on the last page.

ISBN: 978-1-9822-8728-3 (sc)
ISBN: 978-1-9822-8729-0 (e)

Balboa Press rev. date: 07/12/2023

Words from the Author

This book has been around ten years in the making and for that I feel I must apologise, but my spirit guides tell me there is nothing to apologise for as time is of no consequence in the realms of spirituality.

I welcome anyone, spiritual or non-spiritual to read this book. If you are not a believer in the realms of spirit then please read with an open-mind and an open heart. I came to my spiritual journey late in life: around my mid forties, and knowing what I know now about spirit, they will always awaken you by whatever measures are necessary and they will continue to do so until you are on the right path. Let me explain how this happened for me.

Up until this point, my life had been fairly successful. On a work level, I had worked my way through teaching and management and was now a head teacher. I take my hat off to anyone who follows this path; it is extremely stressful and all consuming but can also be so rewarding. I thank all of the people who supported me in this part of my life. I believe that many of the lessons I learned during this time, however difficult, have truly helped me become the person I am today.

On a family level, I have an amazing, totally understanding partner and two beautiful children, adults now, but always my children. Unfortunately, the relationship I had with the father of my children, whom I loved dearly, was destroying all of our lives and I made the extremely difficult decision to walk away from our marriage. In the years after we separated and finally divorced, I was not only in my extremely stressful job, but I was also trying to protect my children from their father, who found it very difficult to manage his own life and therefore was not able to give them the love and stability that they needed. I don't tell you this in the hope of gaining your sympathy; it is a story in a long line of stories that we gather on our Earthly journey. The reason I tell you is, so that I can get to the time in my life when I was truly awakened to the truth of spriitualism and how it can impact on all of our lives..

In 2008, My ex-husband, father of my children, died in very sad circumstances, in fact sad is not a strong enough adjective. The police officer pre-warned me that what he was about to tell me was difficult to say and that therefore, I may find it difficult to take. I still remember clearly to this day my naive response: "You can tell me the whole story, I did my grieving for my husband when we separated all those years ago, nothing you can tell me now will be as bad."

How wrong I was! John died in his bath, fully clothed. We have no idea why he was in the bath although I was told later that sometimes people who are suffering from a heart attack find it the most comfortable place to be. However, we are unsure of the cause of John's death as the police were called to his flat due his neighbour reporting a terrible smell coming from within. I do not wish to go into the details of this, but I tell you to let you know that this event started the journey that I am now on and I thank John, most days, for playing a part in this journey.

After the police officer told me the gist of this, I was indeed traumatised and work had to be put on hold for a while. Whilst out for a walk during my time out, I walked past a little shop in my hometown, which was advertising spiritual readings, I was drawn to book one and the rest as they say is history!

The gentleman who gave me my reading was amazing, he told me things about John, gave me messages from John; things that only I knew; things about his funeral that, at that point, was only in the planning stages and he left me feeling that there must be a huge amount of truth in this spirituality business.

A few months later I signed up for the same gentleman's spiritual development classes and since then I have never looked back. I have come to some abrupt halts and some human traffic jams along the way, but my journey is continuing and will continue forever.

The first few years of this journey were spent with an amazing group of people, where I became able to channel spirit, to give spiritual healing and to sit in trance, as well as many other insightful adventures in the world of spirit. We met regularly to sit in Circle and it was during this time that I developed the ability to write for spirit. The main spirit to work through me at that time was Mary, the mother of Jesus Christ and it is her story that forms the first part of this book, which was written during my time at 'the sanctuary' (the shortened name of the place where I first formed my spiritual friendships both on the Earth plane and beyond).

Around 2013, I stopped writing as regularly and life began to change for me on a human level, which of course impacted on my spiritual pathway. I left the place I had thought of as my spiritual home - 'the sanctuary' - by this point in my own journey I had experienced some amazing spiritual awakenings but also, I was realising that human ego can and does destroy the spiritual journey. Having reflected on this point in my life, I now know that this is why I left 'the sanctuary' and actually took time away from all things spiritual.

Now almost 10 years later it is time to reignite the light within. Don't get me wrong, it has always been there and I have been occasionally allowing myself to be more spiritual again. Now that the light is well and truly back on, it is time to ensure that these words are shared with others and that this 'book' is finished. So here goes!

NB It is worth noting that when I write, I actually close my eyes to begin with in order to allow spirit to merge with my energy, if you could see what my writing looks like you would get a true sense of different energies coming through.

Examples of channeled writing
from the author's notebook

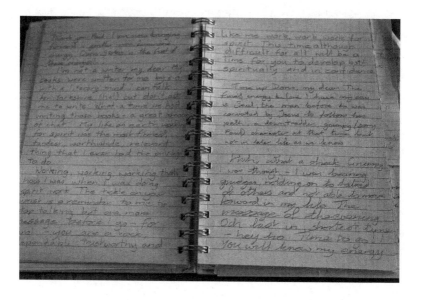

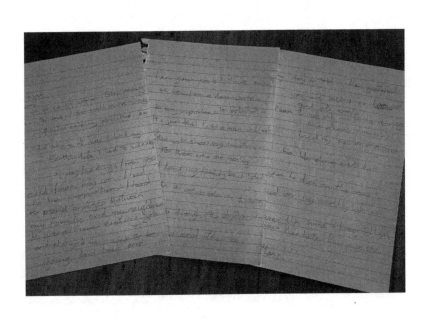

A Message from Spirit

1ˢᵗ May 2017

I have had that 'sixth sense' feeling that I am meant to write again for spirit so here goes...

Dear Spirit,
I am your vessel; please tell me what you need me/others to know.

"You have seen with your own eyes, my child how the word of spirit can end up in print - be brave – this is the next part of your journey. Many have done it before you and with their help and ours, you can too. We want the world to know of our love and also our sadness.

Knowing how to love as we do, with all of your heart, forgiving, joyfully and with no need for reward will help save our mother Earth.

Knowing our sadness for the freewill that is destroying Mother Earth will help save your planet for future generations.

Your book will be full of our words. Your book will focus on how to save Mother Earth and how to bring the people of the world together in loving harmonious relationships. I can sense your lack of belief, but I know you want this and you know others want the same – small ripples in a big pond will continue on as far as they can until they reach the end of their realms. Your book/our words will do the same. Have faith!'

From Ishmael, messenger and philosopher

PART ONE
THE PAST

Mary and Joseph's Story

Thursday, 7 June 2012

Opening words from Jesus, son of Mary and Joseph,

> "Mary and Joseph were never able to write but will work through this lady more frequently to allow them to record the memories of my life that they never could before.
>
> She **must** take time to ensure that this happens.
>
> I also would like my words recorded but my energy is too strong to work with at this moment in time."

Mary

> Good Evening, my dear. You are an inspiration to me, I want to record my memories, as in the book you are reading at the moment.

At this time I was reading 'Iris and Ruby' by Rosie Thomas. The young granddaughter, Ruby, runs away from home and reunites with Iris, her 80-plus year old grandmother. Iris retells the story of her life to Ruby as they begin to build on their relationship. Perhaps Mary was hoping that she and I would form a similar relationship. As this was the first time I had channelled writing in this way, I was full of wonder and hope.

We will work together to record my life and, in turn, that of my son.

I grew up as the middle daughter of a farming family. My father was a diligent man who inspired the village community. As a middle daughter, there were no high expectations for me in terms of education or indeed marriage.

My mother did not always keep well; she worked as hard as she could but it was up to me and my sisters to do the majority of work around the home and farm.

Joseph was not from our village. As a carpenter, he travelled around villages getting work where he could. He would turn up without warning during my younger days and the whole village looked forward to his visits, as he would bring news of the outside world and his many adventures. He was great at story telling and making people laugh. He was also a bit of a philosopher and very good at judging character.

But you are interested in how Joseph and I became a couple...

... I was working in the field one harvest time, basket on back, sun beating down on my fellow workers. We were singing as we worked, most likely because the harvest was good this year (five years before the birth of our Lord Jesus Christ, Son of Man and God). Suddenly, I knew Joseph was there; the bond between us had grown over the years. He was older than I, and in the early years my feelings had been those of a young girl wishing this handsome man would notice and eventually speak to me. I felt the bond between us was strong on my part and hoped beyond hope that I would eventually have the opportunity to meet and share some time with him alone. (The fantasies of a young woman!)

Anyway, back to this day in the field, I was very aware of Joseph's arrival. As usual the young children were running and cheering, gathering around him to welcome him back to our village.

Time is running out my dear – the next instalment will come when you tune in again...You will get more of my story up to the time of Jesus' birth and then Joseph will also give his version. He will speak in a different way and give the same story but from his point of view. This is a wonderful opportunity. Please let it continue. While they are talking, we could continue.

I was channelling all of the above during a clairvoyance class. In this class, one student was giving a spiritual reading to an invited guest while everyone else was writing their messages to share with the guest once the reading was completed. It was during these classes that I started to write for whoever was invited and then realised I was actually getting other messages too. I began to concentrate on writing those instead and now here was Mary, the first spirit energy who came through to give me a full story. I am indeed extremely privileged to be chosen to do this and as she says above we wrote until everyone was finished speaking.

The hay (as you would call it) was swaying in the breeze and Joseph looked over, directly at me, and smiled. That summer I was old enough to know that I was a woman (if you know what I mean!) My mother and father were beginning to look for a husband for me. My older sister had been given to a neighbouring farmer last year and now their attention had turned to me. This summer would be my last chance to get Joseph to notice me, by next year I would be gone from here.

Without all of the detail, there is no need because you all know the outcome, Joseph and I spent many hours in each other's company that summer, always within the confines of family and friends, as it was in those days.

It was coming to the time when Joseph would have to leave. Neither of us wanted this time to come, but come it must.

On his last afternoon in our village, he plucked up courage to meet with my father and ask him if I could become his betrothed. This was a great honour on my family, a carpenter, skilled in his trade, asking for the hand of a farmer's daughter. How could he refuse?

But refuse he did! He told Joseph if he were serious, he would need to stop travelling and settle down. A brave thing (almost stupid, in my opinion!) for my father to demand! Joseph left the next day and I was distraught. This feeling of devastation stayed with me for weeks. (You know that Joseph came back. If he didn't the story would be ending now!)

Six long weeks later, he arrived, strode straight up to my father and asked him to follow him. He had built a house in the neighbouring village (Nazareth). My father disappeared with Joseph and came back two days later (neighbouring does not mean the same as it does nowadays) and it was only when they returned that I found out what he had been doing for the last six weeks.

My father, seeing Joseph's dedication, could not refuse him now. As you can imagine I felt like a queen. The man I wanted to notice me was now to be my husband.

Thursday, 14 June 2012

Mary

Good evening to you all again.
The evening will be quieter tonight but with a lot of laughter. I have a story to tell this evening, which will invoke the same feelings, so back to the fifth century BC.

Joseph and I were not long betrothed; we were both very keen to move to the house built in Nazareth and settle down, so we planned our marriage to take place before the year-end. We began gathering the essentials, including furniture made by Joseph, which he took time over and decorated with love hearts and inscriptions and dates. This furniture stayed with us through out the rest of our lives, such was the quality. When Jesus and his brother were young, they added to the patterns (without being told!) and later with some of the skill of their father.

Our home, when we did move in, was the most beautiful, homely place on Earth, with an abundance of love. Friends and family came frequently to visit and would always ask, in different ways with raised eyebrows and nudging of elbows, when they would hear the patter of tiny feet. Joseph and I, at first, were also very excited and desperate to be able to answer those questions positively. After a few months passed, we became less excited and more despondent.

Where was this baby we so wanted to complete our family circle? Conception was not something I'd though of before marriage. I just presumed I would marry, have a family and love them all for many years. My dreams were not being fulfilled! I prayed every day to our God; my family were Jewish and had always believed in the power of prayer, so this was where I turned at these times. It was difficult to stay faithful in heart as the emptiness of my womb grew and grew to consume my every waking moment.

Joseph and I went between being extremely close and able to comfort each other, to times (which lasted too long due to my stubbornness) of strife, argument and long silences.

Friends stopped asking, family avoided talking about new additions, new nieces and nephews and instead talked about mundane everyday concerns.

Joseph's Story

I am a new energy, stronger, more persistent and straight to the point. I will not give detail and feelings but will add my own philosophy to Mary's words. I will not repeat Mary's story, but I will add to it. So let's go back to what was said last week.

I did indeed fall deeply in love with Mary. She was a gentle soul, obviously in love with me in the shy, coy way women show their emotions.

Her father's refusal brought the message of his love for his daughter straight to me.

I was not going to be allowed to abuse Mary in anyway whatsoever, including leaving her for long periods of time on her own.

I thought on those words and set to finding the perfect place for our home together. In my travels my favourite place was Nazareth. It held many memories of peace, love and companionship. I set to building the home of my dreams, two rooms (most people only had one), with a cooking area including wooden pots carved with love and hope for the future.

Once it was built, it was time to travel back to Mary's family and ask once again for Mary's hand. Mary's father needed to see what I had told him for himself, so we travelled to Nazareth. He was delighted, the agreements were reached and Mary became my wife. Then began the most wonderful time of my life. Everyone should experience love like this once in their lifetime.

As the months went on, Mary became more withdrawn from me and life became very difficult. I did not have 'the faith' that Mary had. She relied on her God for support and guidance; I had no-one. Selfishness was not part of my nature, although many would disagree, given my years of travelling alone. I enjoyed the time that travelling gave me to think and I used my thoughts to change my life.

It was time to talk to Mary.

"Mary, my dearest, I need some time to myself for thinking. I know we always enjoy each other's company and our love is strong enough to overcome these difficulties and I feel if only I could travel for a week or two it would help clear my thoughts and repair our relationship."

She looked at me aghast and ran out of the house in tears. What was I to do now? How could I make this woman I loved see my point of view?"

Mary

He tried over the next few days to explain his thinking to me, but my stubbornness did not allow me to listen. I prayed and prayed and prayed and knew I had to give time to listen to my husband. I loved this man with all of my being and if we wanted our marriage to each other to continue positively, time needed to be given to talking and listening.

Thursday 21 June 2012

Whilst in the clairvoyance class, as previously described, I started to write. This first messenger from Spirit did not introduce themselves as is often the case when mediums connect to Spirit. Perhaps they are just that, messengers, scene setters, but certainly they need to be listened to.

> "Joseph will start this evening's proceedings. Today has been full of highs and lows for this lady. She should not worry; it is a life lesson, but it will **not** affect her professional life."

To clarify the above message, I (referred to by Spirit as "this lady") had received some upsetting news at work, calling my character into disrepute and I was worried about the repercussions. It was reassuring to have spirit channel the above words. As a Headteacher, I often met people who were full of anger, worry and other negative energies as they strived to understand their children's behaviours. It was often the professionals surrounding the child who got the brunt of these negative emotions and the higher up that particular chain you were the more likely you were to get the full torrent of their emotions thrown at you. It can be hard not to take these things personally and, of course, worry that the threats they make will be carried forward. Spirit always find a way to help us through difficult situations in our lives, of that I have no doubt.

Joseph

So here I am, I am not a man of words, I never wrote when I was on the Earth plain and I certainly have no need to do this now. Please correct my mistakes especially spelling and grammar; spoken language has no need of these skills.

We need to carry on from where we left off last time. Mary was very upset with me and didn't speak to me for days. Meals were a slapdash affair. Cold shoulders were the norm throughout the days and weeks. Mary's older sister, Elizabeth came to visit for a while, she too was without child and the two of them just made each other more depressed.

What was I to do? I was despairing! I could do nothing whilst Elizabeth was here because her strength of character and evil eye just made me want to stay out of the way. We had now been married almost a year and our anniversary was going to be a very sad affair if we did not start to speak. I made up my mind to have my say!

I sent Elizabeth back to her husband telling her she had stayed long enough and would never have a child if she continued living with her sister and I. You can just imagine the evil looks I got at that point both from my sister-in-law and my wife! No matter, once I set my mind to a task, I saw it through to the end.

Next, I had to deal with my wife, who was now standing with her hands on her hips, tapping her feet on the ground and ready to explode!

"Don't look at me like that, Goodwife! We have a problem to solve and your stance at this moment will not help!" I took up exactly the same stance directly in front of her and pulled a stupid face.

Mary

"Oh Joseph, how could we have been so stupid?" Both of us burst into fits of laughter and realising how we had been making each other feel; fell into each other's arms. "I am so sorry my love. You know I am a stubborn woman and whilst Elizabeth was here I became even more so. I neglected you, made you feel unwelcome in your own home. I knew I was doing it but couldn't help myself."

Joseph

Mary, you have also, in your stubbornness, helped me to realise a thing or two. I am not a saint. We are both at fault! Your sister has also taught us a lesson. She has been doing the same as I was asking to do; she left her husband to escape and have time to think on her own but now she has returned and I am sure she will be a different person. I do not know if my leaving will help us, but I do know we have a strong, loving relationship, which will not die, no matter if we are apart even for a short while."

We sat down that night and talked and talked and talked- the details are not important, but the outcome is. We agreed that Mary would visit her father for two weeks, after our anniversary and I would have the chance to travel or stay as I wished.

I took Mary to her parents' home and stayed for a day before I left her to be with them, saying I would come back for her in a fortnight.

During that fortnight, I did travel, met up with old friends and spent time thinking. By the end of the fortnight, I had resolved to enjoy my time with Mary, children or no children. We were happy, we could have a loving life together if we made it so.

Mary

I arrived back at our home with Joseph, arm in arm. He had explained how he was thinking and although I knew the yearning in my womb would never disappear, I also knew that Joseph was absolutely correct. We could have a happy life together. He had also suggested that I offer my time to other young mums; giving them the chance for some free time but also giving me the chance to be around children. I told him I'd consider this but wasn't sure that it would help.

It wasn't long before the opportunity to look after children was actually 'shoved in my face' (not my phrase; more Scottish than Nazarene). One of my friends in the village fell when carrying her young two-year old son. She broke her wrist and whilst it was healing I volunteered to help out, which of course, meant looking after Joshua, a beautiful, fair-haired, cherub-like child who melted my heart.

In the evenings, when I returned to our own hearth, Joseph always joked and laughed with me to remind me of all we had together and divert my emotions from being more maudlin.

Joseph

Life continued on like this for the next couple of years, we did have an empty space in our hearts and home, but our love grew deeper and stronger. Every year after our anniversary, it became tradition for Mary to spend a few days with her parents and for me to choose what to do with my time.

Mary

It was a good way to live life, compromising and caring for each other, sharing and solving problems, living and loving and laughing.

Thursday, 9 August 2012

Mary

The emotions I have this evening are slightly quietened. Since you last wrote I have been called to a meeting and reminded of how privileged I am to be able to give you my story. I have to tell you how important it is to keep this story to yourself. I know 'A'. has made you aware of this. The time will come when my story will be made available to all, but time in my world is different to time in your world.

'A' mentioned above by Mary, is the gentleman who gave me my very first reading, as described at the start of my book. He introduced me to spirituality and, at this point in my life, was the person who was guiding my spiritual development.

I left you last time with a story of Elizabeth and her pregnancy. I was very upset, but Joseph, as always, was my rock and we made our way back to where we had been before the news. The next part of the story is so well known that in some ways I feel it is not worth telling but it is **my** story and I have to make people aware of my version of events.

I was at the river washing clothes, singing happily to myself, when the voices which come to me when I pray, became audible in my head. There were no flashing lights, no heavenly host lighting up the sky, just a voice telling me I too would be like Elizabeth; I was with child and the child would follow my God. He was to be brought up as the son of Joseph and I, but he would, through time, be known as the Son of God and we were to call him Jesus.

This was not an immaculate conception, but God, my God, had granted my greatest wish and in doing so I was to be aware of bringing the Son of God into the world. I know what I have just told you is not the way history is written and many religions would be angry if they were to read this. Although Jesus was not an immaculate conception, he was the Son of God incarnate. Our Father God made sure that he came to me from spirit just as those of us, who understand our spiritual essence, believe.

This new information cannot be shared until more people are willing to accept spirituality and the fact that spirit comes to the Earth plane over and over until they have learned the lessons they need.

Jesus was to live his final life on the Earth plane as God's son so that when he transcended to Heaven, he would have the highest position and his closest friends, the disciples, as you know them, would be the hierarchy of the spirit world.

You have a question my child?"

When I am writing, if a thought pops into my mind, spirit can chose to hear it or ignore it! At this point they wanted my question to be heard, so given the opportunity, I asked the following question, which had indeed been in my mind: "If God made Jesus the 'leader' of Heaven 2000 years ago, what was heaven like before then?"

"This is a question to be asked when you feel the time is right."

(Ever felt like you've been dismissed!)

My story is confusing you and you have doubts because of what you have been told about previous writings. This is not an easy task that you have but please persevere. I apologise for giving you this turmoil. You were happier writing about romance and Joseph and I's relationship but the purpose of this story is more important than our love for each other. We will come back to this when you are ready. We will look at Jesus' life on Earth and learn more about what he was trying to do and why.

Thursday, 20 September 2012

Mary

It's a long time since we've 'talked' together my dear. I haven't had the opportunity to meet with you for a while so let's get to work.

The last time we wrote I was pregnant, I have had my beautiful boy now. (No need to go into details of the birth; it is well recorded in many places, although not always accurately!) What are the inaccuracies, I hear you ask? Another time perhaps, I am forbidden to say just now.

My baby boy has given Joseph and I so much joy over the last three years. He plays with the other children in the village while I am surrounded by friends and family throughout the day, and my husband in the evenings. Life is wonderful; the pictures you are seeing in your mind of sandy ground and minimal living is exactly right. Belongings do not matter, health and family are important. Men working to make a living, women washing, cooking and child rearing, children making their own entertainment with stones, sticks, in the river, down ditches, running through fields.

Jesus' younger years were filled with days like this but I always knew he was different. When I prayed, he watched and listened quietly from a very young age. As he grew able to talk, he joined in and as he became independent, he could often be found sitting alone listening. To passers-by he would look like he was not interacting with the world, he was shut off, meditating perhaps. He never used to tell me what was being said to him, but I knew; I got my own messages.

"Your son is meant for greater things, Mary. He will be given a very difficult task to do but do not worry, we are preparing him for the challenges that lie before him. He will always love you but he will grow to love your Father in heaven more. Do not worry about this, you will always be his mother."

You can imagine how these messages set my mind in turmoil, however I kept them to myself. If I had shared them with Joseph, he would have told me to stop havering! I found my own way to accept that Jesus was going to leave - they can't stay boys forever, men have to go and make their own lives.

I put to the side the great things he was going to achieve and the challenges he would face and tried not to dwell on what these could possibly be, I had no knowledge and so why put information in there that might not be right.

So as Jesus grow older, he still played with his friends and they accepted him and all his 'habits', no matter how strange.

Thursday, 25 October 2012

Mary

Good evening my dear, 'long time no see' as would be said nowadays. We really have to increase the meetings we have so that I can give you clear, detailed messages in sequential order with no bits missing. That said, back to where we were last month. Our settlement was in the middle of nowhere compared to towns nowadays. Our roads were different, our transport was different, but we still liked our 'holidays', not annually like most people try to do in your society. I digress!

Joseph and I planned a holiday with Jesus; he was 9 by this time and quite precocious; always asking questions and not the sort that are easy to answer. One day, out of the blue, he asked why the soldiers were doing such cruel things to people. He said, "You know Mum, they really don't deserve to be treated in that way. I feel their pain."

I gave him a hug and remembered what I had been told: "Your son will lead people one day. He will suffer pain and understand the pain of others, so that he can lead with understanding."

As we travelled to the large city, which you know as Jerusalem, the questions continued. Joseph and I laughed and tried to answer as best we could. The journey was fun due to the fact that we were with many others and could spend time together as we travelled and as we camped. Jesus often disappeared to another caravan and could be found 'preaching' to the groups of people who would listen. This would not be many; the children (as children do) found him strange and many of the adults couldn't take to this young boy 'sermonising'. Those that did, however, always came to me to let me know how apt his messages were and how wise; above his years.

Well, as you know my dear, this story heats up when we lost him on the way home. Packing up to go, he wasn't around, but we presumed he was doing his 'preaching' again and carried on packing. As we were about to leave, I went to check who he was with and make sure they were happy to have him with them. I reached the end of the caravan trail without luck but still did not feel the need to panic. I was aware that my Lord would look after Jesus wherever he was and I did not need to be afraid. So instead of panicking, I sat down and prayed, asking my Father God to help me.

I didn't have to wait long for an answer; he pointed me towards the temple where we had worshipped the previous day to give thanks and ask for protection on our journey home. I made my way to the temple with Joseph by my side and I heard him before I saw him. His small gentle voice was resonating around the building and I still remember to this day what I heard:

"You are in my Father's house. He loves each and everyone of us as well as he loves the birds in the trees. In the same way he makes sure the plants, animals, flowers survive in this world. He loves you as much. He does not distinguish between the old, the young, the infirm, the healthy, the rich, the poor; they are all loved equally. So why then do we feel the need to treat people better than animals; the rich better than the poor? Surely the most needy are those that need our love most. Look at yourselves and the way you live, are you living your life the way God wants you to?"

I watched the faces of the holy people in the temple – there were a million stories there! Some in awe; some bewildered; some furious. It was at this point that I felt the urge to move forward, collect my son and leave. Jesus left quietly with his father and I. Moments like that continued throughout his life. His teenage years were full of angst – another story for another time!

Tuesday, 6 November 2012 (5.25pm)

I've no idea why I was made to note the time at the start and at the end of writing this piece, but perhaps it was to let me know that I was not giving enough time to this task and that in reality giving up 30 minutes per day should be easy. You'll note as you read on, how bad I was at listening to Spirit and yet still they persevere.

Mary

> Why have you been procrastinating my child? I am here and ready to talk and now we won't have long before we are interrupted!
>
> This is a lovely room, peaceful and serene like my character. You are not so peaceful and serene but are becoming more so. My serenity is what helped Jesus to be accepted in his young life. He spent many days isolated from his peers and although they were confused by his behaviours, their mothers knew that I was a trustworthy person who could be relied on to give good advice and a listening ear, whatever was required. So, with this and with Joseph's ability to ground people; make them see things for what they really are and not what they might be, Jesus' younger days passed in peace and harmony most of the time.
>
> He had very high expectations however, and often challenged our ways, our thinking and our guidance. There was one day in particular which

sticks out in memory, Joseph was away for a few days working in a neighbouring village and Jesus had been left a list of chores to complete for his father. He was around twelve at the time.

His schooling consisted of listening and debating with the elders in the village as well as learning the Arabic script required to communicate in temples, but not in daily life. He came home from this one day to start on his chores, but came to me first, stating that his Father wanted him to do something more important. Fixing and mending could wait his Father wanted him to persuade the people to follow him. I listened, confused, Joseph, his father, had left him a list of practical tasks and did not expect him to waste time chatting to others- that was what school was for. I said as much to Jesus and he looked at me blankly and said,
"My Father has many roles he wishes me to fulfil and each one is as important as any other. Today it is my duty to speak to the people about my Father's wishes. Tomorrow may be about completing chores, I do not know but I must do as I am asked because only my Father can command me in this way."

And with this said, he walked out into the setting sun and sat amongst the village elders, asking, "Who here will listen to the words of a mere child with much to learn about the world? Who here will willingly accept that I have a message to share and wish to do so with you, my fellow villagers?"

Well, you can imagine, a 12-year-old boy commanding an audience! But, as is always the way with Jesus, he got an audience and started to speak. He spoke about his Father's house having many rooms and that there was space for everyone who wished to follow him there. In these rooms there was much to learn about life and the way of the world. Compassion, sincerity, freedom of speech, the ability to see good in each and every one – lessons that we all need to learn and practise in our daily lives.

I was at one with his message, especially once I understood that he meant his Father God and not his father, Joseph! All was well with me. The elders of the village, however, were confused and spent many hours debating and questioning many issues, including Jesus' ability to speak so eloquently at such a young age; the true meaning behind his messages and of course, whether they should accept the words of a 12yearold boy, not yet a man.

As I have said previously, there were many such episodes as this and with each one Jesus (and his family) faced ridicule, questioning and very little acceptance. As time went on and the years passed it became more and more difficult to protect him and ourselves from human emotions. Never once did Jesus falter from his path and I stood at his side every step of the way.

His father, however, well he will tell you his own story." (5.55pm)

Thursday, 22 November 2012

Mary

> I am trying to get Joseph to come forward to speak but he is very reticent! See, he won't let you keep your eyes closed as he knows this will take you deeper and more accepting/susceptible to his word. Try again, my dear.

When I begin channelling for writing I always start with my eyes closed, in meditation, it allows the energy to begin to flow through me. Sometimes I can write full pages in this manner and always seem to know when to move to a new line, although the writing can be very difficult to decipher, as you will have noted in the photographs of channelled writing, found at the start of this book.

Joseph

> What a stubborn woman my wife is. I really do not want to tell my story and even in Spirit we are entitled to our privacy. All I will say is I was not in favour of Jesus' lifestyle. He annoyed me on many occasions with his apparent lack of respect for his elders."

Mary

> See that wasn't so bad, my darling and I understand your feelings. Now that you and I have returned to Spirit, you know that your Earthly views were

'wrong'. This is the same path as many humans had to take and you can help them as they change their beliefs here and in Spirit."

Joseph

Oh be quiet woman! Stop pandering to me! I am well aware of my Earthly faults and my abilities. I am also aware of how I lived my Earthly life, I had to hide my feelings from you and from my son. I had to be supportive. I had to mend bridges between my family and my neighbours. It was a never-ending job and it changed me. I used to be outgoing, laid back and full of confidence when I met you, Mary, but in the years before Joseph was born we needed to be more supportive of each other and I lost some of my impulsiveness.

Mary

I know my darling, but I loved you for the person you were and the person you became. You were, and still are my rock. Jesus was our undoing in some ways. We tried to be supportive of each other and we didn't really manage as well as we would have liked. I never stopped loving you but I knew Jesus needed me more. You are strong, capable and... I am so sorry.

Joseph put his arms around Mary to console her and wipe away her tears.

Joseph

I am your rock! You are mine! We were and still are a team. Jesus is very important to both of us. It's just that I, as a man, will not/did not show my emotions. For those who are reading this, I loved my family, but I did not take an active role in helping Jesus through the difficult times and this is what embarrasses me, and makes me annoyed with myself."

Mary

I know how you felt and I know that you would always be there, if I needed you. Your relationship with our son was typical of fathers and sons in those days. Fathers looked to their sons to follow in their footsteps and you realised Jesus was not going to do this and as this realisation grew between you, so you grew apart.

Joseph

And there she goes! The story is out now! Don't you just always get your own way woman! There is nothing left for me to say. My story is told and I am grateful you have told it, as I am not great with words. Please do not ask me to do this again and please remember, I loved my son and suffered his life along with him. When he died on the cross, I died too, my Earthly life was never the same. I may tell you about that later but in my time, Mary!

Thursday, 29 November 2012

Joseph

> Ah, good evening. I have come to apologise for my mood last week, Mary was making me do something that needed to be done and I accept that now. We are loving and caring towards each other all the time and last week was not a good place for me to be. I am normally thoughtful and sensitive to others, but I am also a realist; life on the Earth plane is short and needs to be lived to the full. I am ready to work with you my dear, but you need to stop and take time to listen and follow your spirit guides. You are not giving time to this work. Your paid work is important, but we will look after you when you move on. The doctor will tell you that you are stressed and must take a break to rethink, restart. DO IT!

Well, Joseph really gave it to me that night! He was right; as a Head Teacher I was always stressed and sometimes events in my life took over from my Spiritual work. Did I listen to Joseph? Unfortunately not! Over the next ten years I would continue to choose work, family, hobbies over developing my Spiritual abilities more fully. I dipped in and out of my mediumship and my ability to channel writing from Spirit but now 10 years later I hope I have finally reached a point where I will embrace the work that I am on this Earth to do and at this moment that means continuing to transcribe my writing from notes to PC in the hope that they will one day be read and the human race will find them enlightening for the journey we need to make - ensuring Earth survives and evolves. Anyway, enough about me and back to the transcribing. ....

Wednesday, 30 January 2013

Mary

Good Evening, at last! I waited patiently but this has been a long time coming- months since I last wrote to you all. You have to tune out from family, ailments, other spirit energies and give me your full attention, my dear. Close your eyes and let me in...

Well, where did we stop? What if I tell you about Jesus' first independent adventure from the family home? He came to me one day to warn me he would be leaving soon but didn't know when. He said I must prepare and not worry!

A few weeks later I awoke to an empty house; Joseph was off on his venture and Jesus' bed was empty. He had packed some foodstuffs and his warm cloak. The emptiness and loneliness I felt was overwhelming, but I did not worry. I busied myself with the usual chores and when friends asked about my son's absence, I told them' "Like father like son!" My relationship with Joseph was as strong as ever and therefore they believed me.

Eventually, two weeks later, Jesus returned, unshaven, tired and looking like he had not eaten for days. I sat him down to some broth and waited until he was ready to speak. I was biting my tongue but remained quiet. When he talked it was in snippets, which I pieced together as follows:

"Our Father in Heaven has proved His love to me. He has more love for everyone than you could possibly imagine. The tiniest insect, blade of grass, clouds in the sky are counted for and blessed. Not one thing on Earth has been forgotten. I am overwhelmed by the love he has for us, Mother. I must do his bidding. I must be ready to leave and go out in the world. I will have to face many difficulties before I can live my life in the way that God would want me to and I need to move forward in a way that will help. More solitude, more meditation, more thinking time.

Mother, this will be difficult for all us. Your faith will see you through, but I worry about my father. He does not have our faith. He is, however, a strong man and if you don't support him through this he will spend more and more time on his own than he will with you.

I am not going to follow in my father's footsteps. I am going to travel and spread the love of my father in spirit to as many people as I can. I have many years ahead to prepare for this and I will need your support, Mother."

As I listened to this, I accepted more than I previously thought I would be able to. While my son had been away I, myself, had been prepared by our Father in spirit, to accept whatever I was told. As a mother, we want what's best for our families, but who are we to actually decide what might be? My son was happy, his life was full and he was doing a very important job- what more can we ask?"

Thursday, 21 March 2013

Mary

Welcome my dear, it is too long since we last met; 4/5 weeks in your time, a blink of an eye in mine.

You have been worrying so much and I have been worried about you, that is why I have not come close to you. I know you were looking for support and comfort, but you needed to be tested both in your own resolve and in your belief in Spirit.

Neither faltered! Well not too much anyway! Take care. You are doing the right thing and the choices you are making are indeed correct. Try to stop worrying, your path is mapped out and you will be looked after as you journey along.

The people in your company have their own worries and problems and we are looking after all of them, hence the reason for changing guides and helpers as well as energies. Everyone in spirit world respects the work you do to fulfil our wishes.

There is no story from Jesus' life tonight, you need to hear from us and be reassured, you are not the only one who has felt deserted recently. This was not intentional, just a blip, rather like a power cut and due again to changes in the way we want people to work."

Tuesday, 16 April 2013

Mary

You do not need to be in the Sanctuary to write, my dear. You have feelings of loneliness today and yet these are precious moments, time for thinking, for weighing up, deliberating and of course, resting. Whilst it is windy and yet quiet outside, you would not get the same solitude you are getting now. Continue to sleep well, to rest long and to think of your future, all answers will be revealed. The signs are there for you to find them.

You really have no understanding of how ill you are now, you were so healthy before your operation and this step is so different, so unnatural to you. Being unwell is not something you have to face often but this is the height of your illness thereafter there is only recovery.

Time to go and let you recover x"

At this point in my life, I had just had a hysterectomy and was unable to get to the Sanctuary. Thankfully, Mary reassured me that I can channel her energy anywhere; up until this point I had only been channeling within the development classes at the Sanctuary. Perhaps this would now mean that I would find the time to write more frequently. We'll see!

Thursday, 13 June 2013

Mary

My goodness, such a long, long time since we have been together; I feel your delight, I too am excited. I was giving you the headaches this afternoon, changing your energy so that we could work together.

Let's continue the story from where we left off, I know you can't remember but I am scanning your previous notes. Oh yes, Jesus went off into the desert similarly to as described in the Bible. When he came back, he was no longer a boy, and his character had changed, he was more confident, more determined and more able to explain his vocation in life.

"Mother", he would say, "I am my own man, but I will take guidance from our Father above and he will lead me on the right path. I no longer need to take messages from you. I know this will upset you but, when boys become men they no longer need their mother's guidance, they do however, always continue to need their love. Please never stop loving me, mother. My life will be hard for me to live but for you to stand by and watch will be just as difficult, if not more so!"

My son was often profound in his speech and left me dumbstruck on many occasions, but I also reflected on his words afterwards and was able to prepare myself for the future, which by all accounts, was going to be difficult. I smile to myself as I say these words because of course, you already know the way my life was to go, so let's move swiftly forward and I will give my perspective on the events in Jesus' life that you know.

When he left on his travels as I called them, I was of course devastated. My only son, leaving! I had tried to prepare myself, but the actual reality of the event was more traumatic. I remained calm in front of him but when Joseph came home that evening, I was a wreck (as you would say nowadays).

In our time, the days and weeks disappeared without communication, even months and years. I was luckier than most mothers because Jesus became so well known for his stories and talks with others that I often heard of him rather than from him.

I will tell you more of this later, my dear. That is enough for one night."

Sunday, 21 July 2013

During a cruise to the 'Holy Land' I had been told that Mary would make her presence known whilst we were travelling – the following excerpts are from that time. We visitied Jerusalem, Bethlehem, Gethsemane, Golgotha and the many sights which have significance to both the Christian and Jewish faiths.

Thursday, 25 July 2013

Mary

> Feel the love and harmony that surrounds you even in this war-torn country, we will be with you throughout your time in this land.

Mary's Reflections on the 'Holy Land'

Thursday, 15 August 2013

Mary

Let's retrace our steps and I will give specific memories from my viewpoint.

I wasn't with my son for many of his journeys to Jerusalem. Bethlehem, however, is dear to my heart, which mother would not remember the place of their child's birth. The Church of the Nativity, as it is now called, was and still is a very spiritual place. Many spirits congregate there just as the tourists on the Earth plane.

The clearest orbs in the photograph taken in that building are the disciples, they guard the place where Jesus was born. The clearest of all orbs is me."

I visit the place of Jesus' birth often, but it is the place of his death and burial that is difficult to visit, even now. As you know, I was aware that Jesus' life would be difficult but the anguish and sorrow that I felt during his last days on Earth were unbearable. I lost my faith after my son died and it took a very long time to trust in our Father again. When I did however, it was the best thing I did, as of course, it meant Jesus could speak to me.

I have been in the bad books since Sunday, interrupting a healing circle, I should've known better, but I wanted to let you know and thank you. It is one thing to visit these places, using my spiritual aura but to walk with you and share in the experiences that you had firsthand was so real, so different. I know you felt disappointed in the sights as much had changed, it was my disappointment that you felt; the sites have changed, as they should over time and the 'relics' are no longer.

The visit to Golgotha/Calvary, touching the stone where the cross stood, was unbearable. I had to be pulled away from the bottom of the cross eventually but not until Jesus died, I would not leave him in that agony without knowing that I was with him to the end.

In the Church of the Annunciation, the crypt was where the most energy could be felt. Although the priests and keepers of the church are corrupt, the kudos and power were taken over by the love and true message of Jesus on Earth.

Your holiday was only the start of a journey, you need to read more historical and geographical books that will further explain your visit and the sights you saw. I am sorry you didn't feel me with you as much as you would have hoped for, were prepared for, but your energy still needs to adjust, the heat and also the busyness had to be overcome.

Keep trying to work on your meditation, so that we can work on your energies whilst you rest.

I cannot over emphasise the torture I faced as Jesus was put to trial and to death; how can a mother bear this? His burial, at the time, was a period of trance for me, I went through the rituals without thought, methodically. Andrew was the strength at this time, he took control and led us all through it.

Thank you for letting me work with you and apologies for Sunday.

Mary's apology was due to the fact that during a healing circle at the Sanctuary, she had channelled through me (using voice this time); apparently this should not have happened as we were working with members of the public and had no idea of the depth of their spiritual belief. I hope they didn't go away thinking what a bunch of crazies we are!

Thursday, 19 September 2013

I was unsure whether to include ths next section within my book as it is not part of Mary and Joseph's life story, however it appears it has to stay in order to help you, the reader, realise that many spirit energies have gone into the writing of this book and ALL spirit energies are extremely excited to share their stories too- below is a very small example of words from some of these souls.

Mary

> I'm so glad you're here again and writing. (Too many long gaps.) I am going to bring in many different spirit energies tonight. I will tell you who they are so that you can get used to and connect with their energies.
> The first person is Paul, a strong, determined energy, who takes no nonsense..."

Paul: "Good evening, my child, you have worked with me before but only once. I want to discuss with you my writings after Jesus died. 1st Corinthians 4:11 - read it and share it with others. Love is important, people are important to each other, when they retire from life and live alone, they become less loved. It is the job of spiritual people to reach out to people like this."

1st Corinthians 4:11 "To this very hour we go hungry and thirsty, we are in rags, we are brutally treated, we are homeless."

Mary

"Thank you, Paul. I am now bringing forward a gentler, more feminine energy. Doris Stokes is the first of these energies."

Doris: "I'm not a writer my dear. My books were written for me by someone with a literary mind. I can talk for Yorkshire (Ha!) but don't ask me to write. What a time we had writing those books, a great amount of chat. My life on Earth working for spirit was the finest, fondest, most worthwhile, relevant thing that I ever had the privilege to do."

Mary

"Time up Doris, my dear. The final energy before I have my say is Saul, the man before he was converted by Jesus to follow his path, a downtrodden, grumpy (sorry Paul) character at that time but not in later life as we know."

Saul: "Huh! What a cheek! Grumpy I was though, bearing grudges, holding on to hatred of others and not able to move forward in my life - the message of the evening! Och! Last in, shortest time! Hey ho time to go! You will know my energy next time though!"

Mary

"Poor Paul/Saul! Just a wee taster of things to come my dear. You will meditate, write and learn from many new energies in spirit to help you develop your spiritual path. (The scoring out should stay in your book – it shows that you will make mistakes along the way. We all did/do!)

God bless my dear and take care of all in the sanctuary."

Thursday, 31 October 2013

Mary

Life is good when you think positively; I have helped you with this.

Where did we get to with our stories? You are not up to speed with your typing, you have lost your oomph and are not connecting with spirit as well as you need to - speak more to me! Meditate more and your life will be even more enriched.

Now to continue our story; Jesus left the family home and started his journeys around Galilee as you know, he visited occasionally but not as often as his mother would want. I did get news of his life from the many people who passed through the village and all who came sought me out, as if I was something special. Jesus had told them to visit to make me aware of where he was and what was happening, albeit that the information was two sometimes three weeks out of date.

I remember, one day I was washing clothes by the river when a young woman came to visit.

"Jesus is a credit to you, Mary," she said. "Crowds are following him and hanging on to his every word, I have never seen anything like that before. He is more sought after than the High Priests in the temple."

"He has a close group of confidantes who stay close to him night and day. The one that stands out to me is a tall, broad man, called Simon Peter. He seems to be in charge when Jesus is alone, which he often wants to be, especially after long days of answering questions and telling stories."

"His stories always have a lot of meaning for people but are also open to interpretation and questions."

I could have listened to this young lady all day, as she told me about my son, his popularity and his character, his friendships and of course, his life now. What mother wouldn't? Many people when they come to see me just want to make the connection and see the mother of this man whom they hold in awe. Once they see how ordinary I am, they leave fairly unimpressed, but this young woman wanted to connect to both of us and ensure the family joined together again.

You may have guessed by now but if not, this was the Mary who stayed by Jesus' and my side for the rest of his and my life. She was to become my rock. She kept the link strong between us and when Joseph passed, she helped me visit and follow my son.

I will tell you about Joseph's passing next time.

In Love and Light x"

Wednesday, 25 January 2023 (Ten Years Later)

"Mary! Wow! Thank you for coming back. Sorry I have not been available to you recently but as I have discovered since last we spoke; time has no relevance to Spirit, so really, I suppose, there is no need for an apology. Please tell me what you would like me to write today."

Mary

> Good Afternoon (well it is in your time zone!), it is indeed nice to talk to you again.
>
> I will try to start where we left off, telling you about Joseph's death. He really was my soul mate, my angel on Earth and therefore when he left the physical to return to Source I was devastated, but let's remember this is not about me. This is about the events surrounding Joseph's death.
>
> He is not mentioned much in the Bible because to the modern-day church he had no use to them – he lived a quiet life and when Jesus began travelling and telling his story; Joseph did not want to be involved. He loved his son dearly but in his traditional way, he could not understand what was happening. He knew his son was different, he knew the path he was going to follow was not the usual 'father hands down to son' path and he fervently wished it could be that simple.

So, we know already that this was the case and hence Joseph had no inclination to follow his son around the countryside, to all intents and purposes he felt let down by his son.

When we were together, as a couple, I constantly updated Joseph on his son's adventure and he did enjoy hearing what he was doing and how people seemed to love what he had to say, however he had definitely lost a part of himself and his attitude to life became more reserved, less willing to be involved, possibly he was embarrassed that he had not managed (in his eyes) to raise a 'normal' son. Nowadays you would question this view of normality but in the time span that we lived on Earth, traditions were important and meant to be upheld.

So, Joseph, you ask, what became of him?

He did not live to see his son persecuted, so thankfully for him, he left the Earth plane before Jesus was crucified. This may also help people understand why he is not mentioned in the Bible at this most significant time in the Christian calendar and why he is portrayed as a non-event in Jesus' life. Joseph and I both know the true story and both of us are content with our roles in Jesus' life. After all, those roles were as we planned they would be before we reincarnated to that timeframe on Earth.

Joseph died as he had lived in the latter part of his life, quietly and peacefully, no drama. However, we do want to tell you more about why this is as important as my role in Jesus' life; the impact it had on Jesus and the reason why Joseph chose to live his life in this manner- which he only realized once he returned to whence he had come.

All for another day.

With those words and an image of Mary bowing in prayer to me, her spirit energy diminished.

Friday, 27 January 2023

As I listen to some rock 'n' roll music, I ask spirit to come forward today and guide my writing. What do I need to write for you this afternoon? Come forward and let others hear your voice.

Mary is here again. Thank you Mary.

Mary

Thank you for asking me to come forward, my dear child. Let us begin.

Today I wish to tell you about the impact of our family story on the world. Why us?

Consider our three souls in turn – Jesus, the highest developed of all. Myself, able to receive messages from spirit and striving to live a life as spirit would prefer and Joseph, a young soul, with little knowledge of the Earth plane. We, three, represent some of the general divisions of humanity in terms of their connection to spirit and as such you can use us as an analogy for any timeframe in Earth's existence.

Jesus is representative of those folks on Earth who live a wholesome life, taking only what they need, giving without the need for receiving. Throughout history there have been other highly developed souls on your Earth, Lao Tzu, Buddha, Muhammad, Mother Teresa, Wayne Dyer, to name but a few.

There have been a multitude of others, not so famous but all living a simple life, completely aware of their connection to a higher source. This complete awareness comes from numerous incarnations on the Earth plane as well as the ability to keep that connection (that is with us at birth) fully open at all times. Souls like Jesus were/are in their last incarnation on the Earth plane.

Then there are the folks like me, awakened to the ideas of spirituality, able to understand what is required of them but not always able, or willing to make the sacrifices required to reach the next level of enlightenment. Those people have lived many lives on Earth and have learned many lessons during their passed lives, hence they are able to access those lessons because they understand how to tap into their inner soul.

In Joseph's case, as a soul who has had few visits to Earth, he was not fully aware of his own spirituality. He lived life unconnected to the energy of source, enjoying the love that can be found in human relationships but with limited (if any) understanding or acceptance of his internal energy source.

I am sure you can begin to think of your relatives and friends and assign them to one of the above descriptions based on how developed their souls are appearing in this lifetime on Earth. Are the majority of the souls you know like Joseph? Perhaps there are a few like me and if you are lucky, you have met one Jesus-like person – they are few and far between.

You ask about the souls that do not fit into these descriptions, Yes, it is very worthwhile discussing them but let us also remember that there is no judgment attached to being in one group or another, we are all developing and learning and this is just a part of our soul's journey.

The humans on this Earth who do not love, who do not understand the importance of love, either of themselves or of every living thing, those who are so hell-bent on reinforcing their own ego; these are the souls who veer off their life plan, consumed by the belongings they can have, by the power they try to build, they have free will to chose how they live their lives and so they do! The Hitlers, Putins and others like them were all incarnated on to this planet with a life plan which they chose not to follow- this is the downfall of living an Earthly life.

With this in mind, your reader is now ready to consider the next part of your book and now I'm sure you understand that you could not have written these last installments until you had further awakened your soul, hence the reason that this last section of this part of your book took ten years to bear fruit. The journey to the awakening of the soul takes as long as it takes – or not!"

PART TWO
THE FUTURE

You may have noticed that the dates in Part One are many years apart, what happened in October 2013 to stop me writing so abruptly?

LIFE and being human I think. As previously said, it was around this time I left the sanctuary as I felt that ego was in the way of people's spiritual development. I still do and always will believe in spirit and our souls' connection with what some people call the Divine Source; you may call it God, Buddha, Allah but whatever it is, it is a definite energy that draws us to question why we are here, living the life we live.

Between 2013 and now (2022), I have visited a variety of spiritual churches and met many amazing people who fully believe in the world of spirit and the ability to speak to those who used to live on this planet, but recently I have also had the opportunity to explore the idea that there is more to this planet than this planet!

As I began channelling the words of spirit again, I asked that Mary would reconnect with me and finish her story and as you have read in Part 1, she did indeed fulfil my request. This second section of my book takes us from the past into what is in store for us; many excerpts of the channelled writing come from the spiritual realms beyond our own Earth.

19th December 2022

It's taken me a while to get back to this, although in spiritual time it is but the blink of an eye. I thank the Tao and the energy of the cosmos for pushing me to pick up my pen and close my eyes.

Here goes...

"Where have you been? We've missed you but knew eventually you'd come back. Walking through an avenue of lights as far as the eye can see- the planetarium; our sanctuary; Halls of Wisdom. No matter its name, it is where you began and where you return to after each chosen destiny. You are loved, you are unique, you are inspired and inspiring. We bring you here to help you understand the plethora of information coming your way. We are Acturians. You have met the Pleiadians through the reading you have been doing but we will be your authors. There are many others who wish to meet you - go back again and read more of Garnet's work. The time is now. You are not writing to inspire; you are writing to inform. For inspiration you just open your mouth, the words are within you. All you need is trust.

Who?

Where?

Why?

What next?

We will begin with the who..."

WOW! That was an intense piece of writing and difficult to follow yet again. I had indeed been reading about the Pleiadians on a website, which I was finding hard to digest (www.pleiadians.com Barbara Marciniak); the ideas and views put forward were stretching me out of my comfort zone – just like the views being given here.

I had also read two of Garnet Schulhauser's books – 'Dancing on a Stamp' and 'Dancing Forever with Spirit'. These are the first in a series of five books where Garnet, a retired lawyer meets his Spirit guide Albert and, as he journeys with Albert, he records the messages given to him by many different spirits. Some of these spirits we know from the past, such as Mary and Joseph and some we have never heard of before.

As I started to write the introduction above, I seemed to be in a huge, long corridor, referred to above as the Halls of Wisdom or Akashic records. I believe that, just as many people believe in various types of gods, so too many people are aware of a place that holds all of the knowledge from over the millennia. I also believe that we have had many lives and that we chose where we want to reincarnate each time (our chosen destinies) in order to add to the knowledge within these Halls.

To my small human brain, I think the channeled words above mean that we are about to hear from some extra-terrestrial beings and hopefully get some background into **who** they are, **where** they come from and **why** they are here. With this perhaps they will advise us on how to improve our lives and our appreciation of each other and our planet.

WHO?

The Acturians

Are we ghost-like creatures? Do humans actually see and talk to us? Are we taller than any being ever seen? Are we friendly? So, the questions go on but the answers are not heard.

There are people who know us, some know our physical form, some our intellect and some know both. We are willing to be heard by all, but some are not ready or willing to listen. The ego is still too much to overcome for some.

So who are we?

> We are you! We live with you. We support your development.

> We are not your enemy! We are not your keepers! We are whomever we need to be in order to help those of you who hear us to save your planet (or not).

A lot to take in?

> Of course, it is but bear with us - you need us more than we need you. We are all one, we are all new, we are all old, together we will share the secrets of the millennia so that we can face future millennia.

So who are we?

> We are you! If you want to shine your beautiful light energy on the world you inhabit, we are here to support you do just that.
>
> We live with you! Every day be grateful for your surroundings and your relationships - the positive energies which these emanate are where you will find us living.
>
> We support your development! Your planet and life system has been around for a very long time and yet for you to use, it is but a blip. Every invention, every crisis, every war, every success has been planned and worked towards with our help. You need negative experiences as well as positives to give balance and meaning to your development. Love engenders hate. Peace brings discontent. War brings a love of peace. It is the Yin and Yang of your world. Without the downs there can be no ups. We will support you with every decision (right or wrong, good or bad)."

As I type up this first section of writing from the Acturians, I am still confused and I have some knowledge of spirit! They would make great politicians as every question is left unanswered and seems to go off at a tangent. So where does that leave you the reader. I have the urge to try and decipher what has been said above as I still don't have a clear answer to who they are, but perhaps we should just allow them to develop their story and trust that what comes next will enlighten us further.

WHERE?

21st December 2022

The Acturians

Winter solstice... shortest day... energies abound.

Where are we?

Where did we come from?

Where are we going?

Human questions – the short answer is another question. What does it matter? But matter it does! (to you in your human guise anyway!) So, I will answer your questions in the best way I know how. Your ability to understand will depend on your willingness to understand but here goes...

Where are we? I have already told you where we are – we are among you and within you for just as you are a ball of energy so too are we. Our energies merged a millennium and more ago but only those of you who open up your minds to be involved in more than just your human existence will realise that we are here with you now.

I hear you ask, "Why?" as you always do but let's leave that for now and just answer one question at a time.

Where did we come from? That is again a simple and yet complex question- we came from you, who also came from the Divine Creator. Many of you have your God or gods that you see as divine beings and this is not wrong but there is so much more to understand. The Divine Creator is the source of all energy and as such he/she/it can choose to form that energy in any manner.

It would be naive to believe there is only one planet with life upon it. Why should there be when there are many galaxies out there and each one of them with their own planets and their own stars? In reality, we are from one of those other galaxies but as we have been created, all of us, from the one source, what does it matter where we are from; we are the same. Our energies are one.

Where are we going? Now there is a question indeed. We, the beings who are awakened to the ideas I am sharing, we are going to be able to go wherever we wish. When this Earth no longer sustains human life, we will travel to and be part of the one energy source we came from and we will chose our new life based on what we want to learn next. We will move on together.

For those who have not yet opened up their minds to this knowledge; they are not yet ready to make the same journey. Earth will not be here forever, the human life force that lives here will cease to exist and those who are not awake will not move forward into the light.

So, what will happen to them, I hear you ask? And that is because as a human and a lightworker, you have made connections to these beings and have a place for them in your heart. Let me ask you this, if we are all connected as I said, and if we all come from the same divine energy then why do you worry?

Energy is energy, it will return to where it came from and be reused. Recycled, just as you are striving to do to save this planet (too little, too late, I am afraid). There is no amount of work will save Earth, as it is known at this moment. Too many humans have not opened their hearts and minds to the knowledge that we are all one. If you harm one single person, animal, plant then you harm all of us. We will be allowed to return and try again in a different way or, we will move forward to the new life energy that awaits. This depends on how aware you are willing to become in order to make this happen.

It is time to stop for now. Lots to think about and lots to live up to, if you should choose to do so."

WHY?

17th January 2023

The Acturians

Where are we now? What do you need from us? What do we need from you? The 'why' of the story is what is planned for next so let's begin.

As a lightworker, the why may be easier for you to understand than it is for others, but we will take it step by step. This planet has been here for longer than you can possibly imagine and there are indeed many more planets where 'beings', human or otherwise, can live. Some are more successful than others. The successful planets are those where the people (let's call them that to make it simpler) have learned how to live in peace and with no desire to be more important or wealthier than their neighbours. There are others where creativity is the norm, or where science and technology, or living as one with the plants and trees are important to the planets ability to survive harmoniously.

The Divine Source watches over and gathers information from all of these living, breathing planets but as the energies that are sent to these planets do not have freewill, they are like control planets in a huge, intergalactic experiment. Here on Earth, you have a mixture of all of the above and most importantly, you have freewill. But with freewill comes the ability to make choices and for many the choice will be to go down the easiest path.

Imagine if you will, a difficult situation in your own life. How often did you give in to make living easy? Did you throw money at a problem? Was money an enticement in any choices you made? More often than not, the human race uses money as their reason for doing.

Also, let's consider arguments- small family rifts to large global wars. Are they not all about striving to be 'Top Dog'? How many people win a fight by agreeing to differ; by trying to understand their opponent or even better by walking away when conflict is about to arise, so dousing the flame before it has a chance to ignite?

With these thoughts in mind, you have a more 'wholesome' picture of what Earth is like. The love has been lost in the fight for money. Greed has overtaken in all situations - greed dominates the need to be the best country, the best town, the best home, the best person, because 'best' is seen as the more I own, the more I can boast about, the better I am.

In the successful planets, there is no craving to be anything other than what we already are.

So why are we here, amongst you? We are here to begin to reform Earth before it destroys itself due to this overwhelming need to be better.

Take time to stop and share some kindness. Take time to appreciate what you already have.

We too are lightworkers; our planet is thriving due to our ability to accept ourselves for who we are. We have technology, far in advance of that which we find here, but we cannot share this as we would like, until the people on Earth are ready to accept and use what comes their way without needing to consider: how much it will cost; what profit is to be made; who will benefit the most and how can I be the one in charge? All of this is ego-based, we are here to help enlighten you that ego serves no positive purpose.

Now you ask how? How will we achieve this? It will be difficult and we may not ever achieve it but if we don't then Earth may cease to exist, as you know it. It may become one of the unsuccessful trials in this huge experiment of life in the universe. There are many unsuccessful planets out there, but I am not allowed to dwell on those in the confines of this book."

"Why?" you ask.

"Well would you really want to know your future? It is dependent on how you choose to live your life now; the choices you make can influence a positive future. Knowing the potential outcomes means we are influencing your freewill. We have already shared much and to go any further along this path would be seen as persuasion at least, coercion at most.

We must leave you with the warning and allow you to choose what you will do. Although we are allowed to give you more clues as to what type of choices would help.

WHAT NEXT?

19th January 2023

The Acturians

It is imperative that people on Earth move away from greed and power and move towards a far more loving, caring existence.

Perhaps the readers of this book will be able to influence major change in governments around the world, however the majority will read the above statement and either choose to ignore it or put it in the 'It's Nothing to Do with Me' box.

It is our hope that at least some of you will play your own small part. That you will change your ways and try to be more considerate of the planet you live on and the other energies that share this place with you. Believe that it is okay to start small, in the well-used phrase by Lao Tzu, 'a journey of one thousand miles begins with one step'. You cannot change if you do not begin.

So, you may not be the person to bring peace to the nations of the world but you can try to enhance and influence the world around you.

Be kind!

Be loving!

Be a healer!

On a practical level, every day look to do at least one good deed. This will spread the love, the love of humankind, the love of nature, the love of your planet. Learn to love the simple things; a bird song in the early morning, a glowing sunset in the evening and all of nature in between.

Give thanks and be grateful for all that you have. The clear air that you breathe, the people who come into your life, the plants and animals- learn from them. They ask for nothing, they strive only for the things they need to stay alive and they love without conditions.

Change your attitude to the things in live that you treat with negativity - an adversary at work, an unpopular figure on the television, the homeless person begging for money. Be more accepting, less judgemental. You really have no idea of their story and if you believe, like the author of this book believes, that we plan our life before we even enter the womb, then what right do we have to judge the choices of others. We are all here to learn.

I fear I am lecturing too much. I am very conscious of my need to awaken people to their inner soul and to ask them to revert back to the innocence of children. Remember how you trusted and through that trust you had shelter, food and education. You formed friendships, laughed and played with no concern for what came before and what comes next.

As part of the energy of the divine source, I urge you to find your inner self and awaken to it, so that you can live in the now and be in awe of this moment.

20th January 2023

So where are we going today because I've had the sense that Mary wants to finish her story, especially after reading Garnet's experience of meeting Mary Magdalene in 'Dance of Eternal Rapture' So if I just close my eyes perhaps you'll confirm or not…

"Hi Janice,

I am one of your writing guides; I come forward to help you write today. This book will most definitely be a three-parter but it will be your choice how it is finally written, I would expect that you, being a creature of habit and organisation are unhappy that things have been left hanging, I ask you not to worry, all will be revealed- just go with the flow!"

At this point my writing guide left the scene of my mind, my eyes open and I am no further forward in knowing what's next. I suppose I just have to go with the flow…

PART 3
THE NOW

"I know you expected (wanted even) to go back and fill in the gaps. It is so fortuitous that you feel the necessity because it is a fantastic example of the human brain's need to cross the t's and dot the i's. Have you learned nothing as you delve into your spirituality – TIME IS NOT IMPORTANT! The only important moment is the one you are in right now.

Let me explain by considering each one in turn Past, Future and the Now.

We all have a past, of course we do, and in that past we have hopefully, learned many things and are using what we have learned in this moment, here and now. I cannot emphasise enough the importance of the moment you are in here and now. If you consider a previous argument; the words that were spoken at that time; the hurt that was caused; the emotions that were released; I presume you would like to go back and change it. Well you can't! In that moment the negativity was released and leaves its eternal mark on the Universe.

Now that was just one argument, there are millions of events which have occurred in life that were far more catastrophic, those that have hit the headlines and those that the media did not deem important enough to broadcast. All of them have left their mark on this planet and because we are all connected to each other and to the Divine Source then they have left a mark on each and every one of us.

Do not become too despondent, for just as wars, murders, violence of all sorts leaves a negative mark, so it is only right that the joyous moments from your past also leave lasting positive imprints on all of us.

You may make time to dwell on these moments too; the birth of a child; family celebrations; a kind word or giving freely of your time and talents. Remember the love you felt in your heart at those points. These moments are the most important from your past, not because they fill you with joy now when you think of them but because they also impacted on the energy, which binds us all as one.

Are you envisaging a set of scales, positive on one side, negative on the other? Good! Now what happens when one side gets too heavy?

You cannot return to the past and start changing all of those negatives to positives. You can only add to the scales from your actions at this moment. So can you see the past is not relevant to saving Earth. Only the actions of the Now can be added to the scales.

Of course, if this is the case for the past, then the same must be true for the future; there is no point in wishing for a 'brighter future', unless the work is done now to be bright!

Many humans spend too much time planning for what is to come – a new house, car, job, more money, more influence, the holiday of a lifetime. Why can't they just be happy and content with what they have on a daily basis? Planning ahead, whilst it may help humans deal with this existence that they have chosen; it means that they miss out on so much of what is around them at this moment.

By all means, take time to plan that upcoming holiday but remember to enjoy the planning as much as the holiday itself. How often do people go into debt in order to enjoy a luxury item? Surely, if we learned to be content with living within our means, we could bring so much more joy to not only ourselves but also our planet.

So, I ask you not to get bogged down in future planning; it can also add to the scale of negativity and serves no purpose in the here and now?

I sense your mind is whirring with questions around global warming and the need for governments across the globe to commit to future targets. I answer that with another question-how can you influence the future? Answer- by acting now!

All paths seem to be leading to the same conclusion, the past is gone, the future is not available to you as a human being, therefore, be content in the Now.

The Now is where you live your life. The Now is where your thoughts, words, actions and deeds have the biggest impact. The Now is how you save this planet.

No matter that you are only one person, from this moment forward, strive to be a kind, loving soul and in doing so you will influence others around you to be the same. We know as humans, you will find it difficult to be kind to everyone and everything. You harbour grudges from past events. You decide you dislike a person based on one thing they did years ago and you continue to hold this against them. (Remember the discussion around negativity – let it go, stop bringing more negativity to this moment.)

Be your own responsibility. Claim your actions, words and deeds. You can only change you and the more light you shine onto the world, the more the scales of positivity will overflow.

I could continue writing (well getting you to write for me) on this subject forever, that is how important it is, but I understand the need for humans to be in control of their own destiny, so I leave these musings of an old man with you to do with as you please. You have freewill after all."

Sir Arthur Conan Doyle

23rd January 2023

Okay guys, come forward and inspire me. I need direction and of course, words of wisdom. I know you said to leave the organisation to you, so that is indeed what I must do, because I trust you implicitly. Right now I'm encouraged to write about my journey into telepathy, so here goes...

My sister-in-love and I have a very strong bond and spiritual belief. (In reality she is my sister-in-law but that doesn't do our relationship justice, sister-in-love sounds so much more.) She and I agreed to try and speak to each other via telepathy, the reasons why are embedded within this book. So for the past two weeks (you have to begin somewhere!) we both sit down to meditate and try to tune in to the other's thoughts at exactly the same time – 8.50am on Monday mornings.

Last Monday, our first try, she apparently tried to send me the image of a strawberry- never happened! However, I did intuit the fact that she was sitting cross-legged on the floor in front of me within a beautiful crystal white light. My vision was of a magnificent heraldic-looking stag, which she said could have come forward because she was watching a movie the previous evening, which had such an animal in it.

Who knows? Were we just trying to make it fit? If you trust in spirit energy and the fact that we are all connected as one- then no, we did not make it fit. We were just like one of those old-fashioned radios, trying to find the right wavelength.

Today when we tried, I thought I was supposed to send an image and she was to try and receive it. What actually happened was that we both sent images and neither of us received them, we did however, again visualize each other sitting cross-legged on the floor, facing one another, I also saw our souls clash in the void (no other word comes to mind to explain it), which was an indescribable purple-blue colour – again Sandra confirmed this was the colour she was meditating to.

As for the images we were trying to send - both of us had chosen pink hearts! Synchronicity or something deeper, more meaningful?

RESPONSE FROM SPIRIT

As I sit down to write this next section it is important to understand that once a connection is made with the energy of those we cannot see, that energy can sometimes become 'a oneness' and therefore, it does not matter where (or who) the words come from, the energy actually has no name on an individual basis but as humans we like to fit things into boxes in order to categorise our knowledge; it helps us to understand and prove existence. The energies that come forward to communicate through me in this final section did not always give a name. I hope, however, that you are still able to understand and utilise the information given.

"So what does all of that prove?" the reader asks and I am here to provide an explanation. Again you must open your heart and be ready to accept. The questions you have, the dismissal you wish to give is fair enough, you are human after all. There are some of you out there who will accept what has just been written and also what I am about to say and you will agree whole-heartedly. There are others who want to belief but will want umpteen layers of proof to ensure the facts and then, of course, there are those who will scoff and ridicule. All I can say is you are all on a journey; some are closer than others to realizing this.

So back to my explanation; as has been previously said we are all 'just' energy and that energy emanates from one source, therefore we are all connected and, as Janice says, if you can get on the same wavelength then it is far easier to communicate with each other in the way described above.

The mention of the 'void' - the space between the space - is again a concept many of you will find hard to comprehend but as energy tries to follow its path to where it is required, any blocks put in its way stagnate the flow and it either dissipates or returns to whence it came or indeed, surges and implodes, therefore the best place for energy to flow freely is in a space where nothing can interrupt it. The 'void' is such a space and it can be reached by emptying the mind and by just being.

What better example can there be of living in the Now?

After writing the initial paragraphs on the Now, Janice was concerned that it was too dictatorial, too demanding. Perhaps she is right, but she worries, from her human ego, that people will be offended, upset by the seriousness of our words.

She may be right; unfortunately, we deal in truths and therefore the message needs to be clear. Hopefully many of you will understand this and begin to change your ways. Perhaps you will meditate more frequently, perhaps you will endeavour to be kinder not only to fellow human beings but also to the plants and animals that share this planet and therefore your energy, perhaps you will be more mindful of living just with what you have and not find the need to strive to prove yourself as better than others.

You are you! You are wonderful! You are created from one source of energy that is pure divine love, how could you not be magnificent? Just open yourself up to believing this and give gratitude every day for what you are, in this moment. Now."

24th January 2023

Having just typed up yesterday's writing, I have had to stop and turn directly to spirit; my misgivings surrounding: "How can **I** be the person to write this book?" are huge.

I am human, I have made many mistakes in my life, fallen out (and back in) with many people and caused hurt along the way. So I stopped, asked for guidance and was told, I can only forgive me and what has been done to me, I cannot expect to **be** forgiven- that is not my choice.

However, my life in this moment is different to that of the past and my life in the future is unknown, so right here, right now, I am loved, I am healthy, I am cared for. Live in this moment now and be the best you can be. By all means learn from the past mistakes but don't dwell on them, nor on how they may impact on your future- it causes more imbalance to those scales.

So with that in mind, I will write the rest of this book with love in my heart so that I can encourage others to be the same.

2nd **February 2023**

I sit to write today after an extremely busy day (for a retiree!) and I can feel spirit nipping my ear - the pain is unbearable – probably because I haven't sat to write for a few days and now, when the time is available I chose to do something else! So here I am! Let's go!

"Oh, you are so difficult to get to this space but also so easy to connect with once you are here. We sense the noise of the wind outside and your thinking brain wonders who I am and what will we write today?

I am Androcoles. It is a pleasure to connect with you. You will find yourself having to stop more often as you write, for my energy is not one you are used to- just breathe through it and we will be fine.

Today we will write about my role in supporting this planet to be much more than it already is. Some humans look at the planet with wonder and sense its beauty, others look with wonder and sense the need to enhance what they have by using what is freely available, others look on in despair at the true state that Earth is in at this moment.

I have been around for many of your Earth years and I have seen the true beauty of it. At its inception, Earth had everything required for life to begin and so there was no need for more. The water was pure, the soil fertile and the air fresh. All life giving.

When humans look at Earth with wonder, they may see the beauty that is all around, because of the three life givers. They are in awe of the delicate intricacy of a butterfly's wings, they sit for hours at the side of a babbling brook, they truly love being able to be outdoors. Furthermore, they look after what they have, they respect the plants that grow, they make room in their own gardens for wildlife and greenery. They embrace all that is good.

Those who sense the need to enhance this wonder that they see around them may not always do this with the intention of making Earth a better place, but more likely they do it with the need to better themselves financially or perhaps to increase their power. I refer, of course, to those who have used what the Earth has to offer by generating a need for fuels taken from the heart of the planet, or by destroying natural landscapes to make way for money making ventures. This is not enhancing Earth in anyway, shape or form!

Those who look in despair, can see both sides of this coin described above, and are extremely aware of what needs to change. These are the people I have previously connected with and enlightened, It is my duty to continue to do this and to help Earthlings turn from destructive paths on to those that can return Mother Earth to its original symbiotic state. I need your help to reach more people. We must encourage everyone to appreciate the natural beauty and wonder of this planet and we must support those who seek power and glory to understand that their life's would be so much better if they released the need for hierarchy and financial gain, learning to live instead, with what Earth can naturally provide.

It is my hope that every person, every day, will waken their minds and more importantly their hearts, to the beauty of this wondrous planet and all that it has to offer.

I leave you with these thoughts to include in your book, wherever you see fit."

Thank you Androcoles. And thanks also for taking away the sore ear!

6th February 2023

I began my writing session today by writing out a load of questions. Jeremy Vine was on in the background (Radio 2) discussing this knew AI app which writes huge paragraphs for you if you just type in the question, so you can imagine the thoughts in my head - who needs me to write a book? Who needs spirit? Who needs books? Really feeling confused today, but if I've learned anything while writing this it is to trust that I am doing what is right and that the answers will come. With that in mind my final question for spirit today is this - What is the message that our book is going to get across to the reader?

"Oh, my goodness, so many questions before we even start today! Let me introduce my energy to you this afternoon – do you feel that calmness, that eternal peace and joy? Those feelings are with me at all times. I am not from your world, where I am from is of no consequence, but what is of consequence is those feelings, continue to enjoy them as you write for me.

You ask why we write this book? What is its purpose, its message? In essence it is to try and encourage the human race to have more love in their hearts, because with continuous love comes continuous contentment and joy- the emotions you are feeling now.

Our race live in complete harmony with each other, no worrying about who is right or wrong, no angst over how others feel towards us and certainly no need to be anything other than who we are. Our planet thrives on the fact that we all have this continuous feeling of peacefulness, of eternal love. We go about our lives knowing completely that everyone we encounter comes with good intentions. No one is out to harm anyone else. All that we do, we do with love in our hearts. Let's imagine a typical day in a human life and let's try to influence some of the activities with continuous love.

The alarm goes off to signify the start of a new day, the human turns over for another snooze before having to face what lies ahead. Imagine, instead that alarm signified the start of a new, love-filled day- wouldn't you just jump out of bed (bad back allowing!) and be thankful for all you are about to experience.

Jumping ahead to breakfast time; the rush to get organised; to get out the door and face the rush hour traffic, thinking of what issues you will be faced with as you complete your daily life. Again, imagine how this would all pan out if you were more relaxed, more in love with the world; would there be such a rush - remember you now get up without that extra snooze? The family would not be complaining because their lunches aren't prepped or the breakfast on offer isn't ready. The commute would be less speedy, less frantic as everyone engages with everyone else with a smile and a pleasant word as well as trusting that things will fall into place.

With the day starting well, so it would continue, colleagues fulfill their work commitments with acceptance. There are no difficult phone calls, no irate clients, no time-wasters or shirkers, nothing to complain about.

Can you see how life would change for the better? And all it takes is love! Surely it is a simple step to take. Why then is this planet suffering? Why is it not able to move towards that place where everyone loves each other?

We have already said that we all come from Source, from that divine, loving energy and yet when we transition to Earth with our Life Plan, which includes acts of kindness and the need to help others, we soon forget the plans we made and revert to an easy life, following the choices which make us happy without considering the impact on others or indeed on this planet.

And there you have your answer – on my planet we are blessed with the ability to remember our Life Plan and where we have originated from. Humans do not have this ability. Choosing to incarnate on Earth is a very difficult choice and we take our hats off (if we ever wore one!) to those souls who chose this planet.

So please, as you read this, do not beat yourself up because you feel unloved, put upon, taken for granted. This is your human life, surrounded by others in the same position. You are reading this book; you have awakened your soul to the knowledge that you are loved by the Universe. You are now able to share that love as best you know how, whilst still trying to offload those negative human traits and emotions; anger, jealousy, bitterness to name but a few. You are still trying to forgive yourself for the poor choices made in your human existence so far; still trying to forgive others for the hurts they have caused you.

Let's finish by remembering you chose this Life Plan and now that you have awakened the need to share love, you can move forward with a light in your heart.

About the Author

Janice is a retired Head Teacher who was awakened to the idea of spirituality after the untimely death of her ex-husband. Prior to this she existed, as others on this planet, in ignorance of the soul's energy within her. During the following years, she has tried, and oft times failed, to be the spiritual beacon of light that Source would want all of us to be. She is a spiritual medium and healer, who has useds this training to give platform demonstrations, private readings, to co-write a training manual for spiritual healing and to train others this art.

Many years ago, she was asked by Spirit to write this book and did indeed channel messages from Spirit at the time. Recently, Spirit once again tried to get her to write, this time with far more success. In a conversation with her 'sister-in-love' she stated that she was not the author of this book and did not want her name on the cover, as the words within are not hers but directly from spirit.

She hopes this book brings more understanding to the life we are living now, and that it improves our ability to love unconditionally.

Printed and bound by CPI Group (UK) Ltd, Croydon, CR0 4YY